MW00388810

BORN BEAUTIFUL

A Mother-Daughter Conversation on Beauty and Identity.

Dear Nannie,
You are fabulous and I love you!
♡ Sara

By

Brittany Frey and Sara Cormany

For All The Girls

We Love

A Note To Our Mamas...

As women, we all know the journey to embracing true beauty is a complicated one. It is often a daily, uphill battle to exchange perfection for His grace and lies for His truth. As mamas, our hearts are often drawn to this exchange as we fight to give our daughters a Jesus-breathed perspective on beauty and identity.

It is this battle that inspired us to write *Born Beautiful,* a 12-week mother/daughter devotional whose purpose is to provide a safe place for both mother and daughter to exchange our image-obsessed culture for God's grace and love. Each week combines our own stories with interactive questions and challenges to help illustrate God's truth in a purposeful way.

While this is meant to be a 12-week journey, we are also real, tell-it-like-it-is mamas. We know all too well that life doesn't go exactly as planned. So, we created a flexible format that could be used over the course of a year and chapters that could be read all in one day or over the course of one week.

In the same way, even though this book was written for moms and daughters (ages 6-12,) the content is also more than applicable to a similar relationship (aunt-niece, grandma-granddaughter, etc.) It is our hope that this flexibility will allow every reader to have the best experience possible.

Happy Reading!

Brit and Sara

Introduction

It was when I was happiest that I longed most. The sweetest thing in all my life has been the longing to find the place where all the beauty came from.

C.S. Lewis[1]

Beauty.

From the moment we draw our first breath, we will long to find it, to chase it, to own it. We will go from store to store, product to product, person to person in the great hope that someday, we'll figure out how to be beautiful enough.

But this longing was never meant to keep us chasing things that will fade away. This longing, this desire to know true beauty comes from our need to find our Heavenly Father.

It is only as we pursue Him, seek Him, and know Him that we will be able to discover "the place where all the beauty comes from." Because it will lead us to the foot of a Cross and offer us the grace of a Son who gave it all so that we could know His Father.

The King of all Kings. The God of the Universe. The Author of All Things.

Any pursuit of the meaning of beauty begins with a Father who loved us so much He gave up His whole world, His Son for the chance to spend forever together.

---

[1] C.S. Lewis, *Till We Have Faces: A Myth Retold,* (United Kingdom: Geoffrey Bles,1956.)

That, dear girls, is where our journey begins.

A place where we can trade the world's definition of beauty for who God says we are in Him. A place where we can celebrate someone else's beauty without questioning our own. A place where we can love one another as He first loved us.

Because *this* is the place we have all been longing to find.

Week 1

I am born beautiful.

"We were created in
the image of our Father,
made on-purpose and
beautiful by
the God of the universe."

Reading Time:

I praise you because I am fearfully and wonderfully made; your works are wonderful, I know that full well.

-Psalm 139:14, NIV

Story Time with Brit:

The second I saw it, I saw nothing but flaws.

The dark circles. The bags underneath my eyes. The vein that always seems to stick out on my forehead. The barely noticeable pimple on my nose.

Each less-than-lovely mark glaring back at me in a photo that was supposed to advertise my new line of fitness t-shirts. A line meant to speak the truth that I am fearfully and wonderfully made, dark circles and all. And yet, somehow, I found myself missing my own message.

Before I knew it, I was flipping through filters on my phone to find the one that made my face "good enough" to post on social media. I took a gifted photographer's work and mangled it with my insecurity. It was not until I found myself apologizing to her for altering the photo that I heard my boy's words echo in my heart, "You were born beautiful, mama."

How many times had my little man taken my face in his hands and spoken this truth over me? How many times had I been reminded that my Father speaks it too? How many times had I spoken that truth to other girls? And here I was doubting *again.*

The battle of seeing ourselves as God sees us is an everyday struggle. Girls struggle. Mamas struggle. We all struggle. It is why we must constantly seek the truth together. And in that seeking, move toward the grace of knowing that God chose us, loves us and we are beautiful in His eyes.

So, let's chase, claim and know His kind of beauty, *together.* Because the end of each day will find us all wanting to hear, "You were born beautiful."

Truth Time:

Exceptional. Extraordinary. Incredible. Tremendous. Mighty. Powerful.

All of these words describe what it is to be made fearfully.

When David, a king from the Old Testament, writes in Psalm 139, "I praise you for I am fearfully and wonderfully made," he is saying that we are all created in an exceptional and extraordinary way. But it isn't enough to simply understand David's words, God intends for us take those words and write them on our hearts.

It is why he follows "I praise you for I am fearfully and wonderfully made" with "your works are wonderful and I know that full well."

He is saying that our lives should reflect the beauty and wonder of our creation. Any time we doubt that or tell ourselves we need a filter to be good enough for the world, we need only to be reminded we were created in the image of our Father, made on-purpose and beautiful by the God of the universe.

It is why God's truth is the only way for us to guard our hearts from a world that will try to make less of our exceptionality.

So, the next time we experience doubt that we were born beautiful, let's speak this truth over our hearts, "We are exceptionally made, extraordinarily crafted, powerfully woven together *by the God of the universe.* We will say this, shout this, sing this until our souls know this FULL well. For we were born beautiful and made for an even more beautiful purpose, to love others so well that they will see in us the God we love with all our hearts."

Girl Time:

Questions to Ask Your Mom:

What is one thing you struggle with when you look at a photograph of yourself? Why? How can you begin to see that differently or as God sees it?

Questions to Ask Your Daughter:

What is one thing you struggle with when you look at a photograph of yourself? Why? How do you think God sees you?

Challenge Time:

Rewrite Psalms 139:14 in your own words. Then share your version with your mom/daughter and talk about how the process helped you to better understand God's truth.

Week 2

I am forever His girl.

"Our stories are meant to be told so that others around us can know what a difference it makes when we live as daughters of a King..."

Reading Time:

For all who are led by the Spirit of God are children of God. So, you have not received a spirit that makes you fearful slaves. Instead, you received God's Spirit when he adopted you as his own children. Now we call him, "Abba, Father." For his Spirit joins with our spirit to affirm that we are God's children. And since we are his children, we are his heirs.

Romans 8:14-17a, NLT

Story Time with Sara:

Early one morning, I awoke to the sound of her pitter patter down the stairs.

A yawn and a stretch later, I clumsily found my way out of bed, only to peek around the corner and find her just as I had the day before.

Her little arms readied in a delicate pose. Her feet steadied only by a two-inch plastic heel. Her head stilled to keep her sparkly tiara secure.

It was as if she was frozen in time.

Frozen until a familiar voice began in a lilting *1-2-3, 1-2-3, 1-2-3* as she melted into a sway and step befitting of the on-screen princess and her *1-2-3.*

I sat down slowly onto the stairs, marveling a bit at my girl.

The one who loved all things sparkly and pink and royal. The one who called her daddy, her prince and her mommy, the queen. The one who imagined herself to be Cinderella and Sleeping Beauty and Fancy Nancy all in one day.

Living as if there was no doubt that she belonged in a place of beauty and significance.

She was a princess and that was that.

But then time passed and tomorrow came. The plastic heels became too small and the tiara too tight. *1-2-3* turned into *4-5-6* and *7-8-9* all the way to *12*, trading sparkly for strong, ball gowns for t-shirts and delicate steps for fierce compassion.

How different she is from the tiny dancer of years ago and yet, she is no less His, no less loved, no less royal.

Because with every step she is becoming who He has made her to be. With every sway, she is moving toward another adventure, another way to love others. With every year, she is using the strength of her voice to tell the story of the best kind of ever-after.

A story where she is forever and always the daughter of a *King.*

Truth Time:

Holy. Chosen. *Accepted.*

Somedays, we may feel unworthy of these words but when we say yes to Jesus, we can know the grace and beauty they offer because the Cross gives us a way to a forever Father.

And in the very the moment we become daughters of God, we are called by Him in a *1-2-3* song that speaks of acceptance. But as we grow, it becomes more and more difficult to dance to that truth with the confidence we have when we are very small.

It is easier to listen to others who say things that make us feel rejected or less than who we know God says we are. It could be as simple as someone at school who refuses to play with us on the playground or sit by us at lunch. But it also could be a more complicated hurt that we carry, brought about by someone who is unkind to us over and over and over again.

The more hurts and harsh words we carry and the longer we carry them, the harder it is to hear the voice of God and yet, we have already forever secured a place of beauty and significance in our Father's heart.

I Peter 2:9-10 says, "But you are the ones chosen by God, chosen for the high calling of priestly work, chosen to be a holy people, God's instruments to do his work and speak out for him, to tell others of the night-and-day difference he made for you–from nothing to something, from rejected to accepted."

Holy, chosen and accepted for *a unique purpose*--to love others as He has loved us, no matter if we are *7-8-9* or *40-41-42.*

Be it in the cafeteria or a coffee shop, our stories are meant to be told so that others around us can know what a difference it makes when we live as daughters of a King, when we accept the grace of Romans 8:14-17, "'We have been adopted by God. The Spirit makes us sons (and daughters) of the Most High God. Because of this, we cry, "Abba, (Daddy) Father.'"

It is in that grace that we are allowed to be who He made us.

T-shirts or ball-gowns. Tennis shoes or tiaras. Sparkly things or sports things.

We are forever *His* girls.

Girl Time:

Questions to ask your mom:

When have you struggled to feel accepted? Were able to replace that feeling with truth? Why or why not?

Questions for your mom to ask you:

As a daughter of a King, you are made to be you. Make a list of all the things that make you, you. If possible, use "I am" statements like the ones used in our chapter titles (e.g. I am funny. I am freckled. I am athletic.)

Challenge Time:

God uses us as His instruments to tell the world the story of a Father's love. Take the time to write the story God is telling in and through you. Find a way to use that story to make a difference in someone else's life.

Week 3

I am never alone.

"He was there, speaking
His grace over me,
'I am with you, my love,
and you will not fall.'"

Reading Time:

Don't panic. I'm with you. There's no need to fear for I'm your God. I'll give you strength. I'll help you. I'll hold you steady, keep a firm grip on you.

Isaiah 41:10, The Message

Story Time with Brit:

My littlest girl was gone.

I knew it the moment I saw the front door standing wide open.

With my heart in my throat, I ran down the stairs shouting out each of my babies' names. I heard my oldest call down from her room. And then my boy, Eli, found me soon after that.

But where was my Lauren?

It had only been ten minutes since I had left all three of them piled onto the couch, sorting through all their Valentine's candy and cards o go upstairs. It had only been ten minutes. But now the front door was open and I couldn't find my sweet girl.

So out of sheer panic, I began to run.

I ran upstairs and down. I ran room to room. I ran out the front door. I ran out the back door. I ran past the pool and the playground. I ran up and down the streets. I ran to every place my mind had determined she could possibly be, screaming helplessly, "Lauren? Where are you, baby?"

When it seemed as if there was no place left to look, I called *911.*

As I began to describe my baby's face to the dispatcher, my mind flooded with all the things that could have happened to her and I was left feeling broken under the weight of possibility.

After what felt like an eternity, the police arrived. As they made their way up to Lauren's room, I sank into the stairs with my hands over my head which now hung in desperation. So, I began to pray a broken prayer of "Jesus, help me. Please, please, Jesus. Help. Me."

Over and over and over again.

In what seemed like only a breath, I heard my oldest begin to scream, "Lauren!" I scrambled to the top of the stairs only to fall on my face weeping with joy.

Lauren was *found.*

My dear girl had been sleeping in her bed the whole time only but her blanket had so completely covered her body that in all of my panic, I just hadn't *seen* her. But now, it didn't even matter. All that was left to do was hug her so tightly it was hard to see where I stopped and she began.

My baby had been *found.*

And somewhere deep in my heart, I knew I hadn't been alone in my fear because Jesus had been there along.

In my running here, there, and everywhere. In my crumpled on the stairs with my head bowed low and my hands held high desperation. In my face to the floor relief that my girl had been found. And in every moment in-between.

He was there, speaking His grace over me, "I am with you, my love, and you will not fall." (Psalm 46:5)

Truth Time:

Panic.

The feeling is undeniable.

The cold rush of adrenaline. The pounding of our hearts. The sweat beading on our hands.

We know we need God more than ever but no matter how hard we try to lean into that need, He feels so incredibly far away.

We will *all* have moments like this when we feel overwhelmed and fearful. But God wants us to know that He is present in every moment, holding, loving, and supporting us. Even when the world feels out of control and we are left feeling helpless because of the circumstance, God is there to steady the storm and offer us peace.

All we need to do is ask and He promises to answer, "Peace I leave with you; my peace I give you. I do not give to you as the world gives. Do not let your hearts be troubled and do not be afraid." (John 14:27)

Even when the asking is a messy "Jesus, please." Even when the searching for what is lost turns into what has already been found. Even when loneliness grasps the heart and nothing is left but to sink into the stairs and wait.

He promises to be there for us all just as He was there for me.

Because even when I felt broken, lost, and alone, God was with me all the way to finding my girl. He was reaching out and pulling me close enough to make me hear His voice, "Don't panic. I'm with you. There's no need to fear for I'm your God. I'll give you strength. I'll help you. I'll hold you steady and keep a firm grip on you." (Isaiah 41:10)

Yes, there will be times when we are afraid. Yes, there will be times when we feel alone and no one else understands. But we can trust that God sees us and He *will not* let us fall.

Girl Time:

Questions to ask your mom:

When have you felt completely paralyzed with fear? Who or what did you turn to during that time?

Questions for your mom to ask you:

What are your greatest fears? How can I encourage you in overcoming those fears?

Challenge Time:

Choose one thing in your life that brings you fear. As mother/daughter, come up with a practical way you can face that fear together. For example, if one of you is afraid of heights, plan a trip to a place that challenges that fear and conquer it together.

Week 4

I am made to do hard things.

"I had finally realized that a body that moves, no matter how fast or how slow, is an absolute gift. And I had to face the fact that I had let one moment steal the joy of living my best life."

Reading Time:

I can do all this through Him who gives me strength.

Philippians 4:13, NIV

Story Time with Sara:

Tears sprang from my eyes as the rhythm of her words pounded into my 8-year-old heart, "C'mon Sara, this isn't a contest of who can be the slowest!!!"

With every eye in the third grade on me, I desperately pushed my legs one after another toward the finish line. A short wheeze and a cough later, it was over. And I could even feel my head raise a little bit higher because slow or no, I had run my mile.

But then her words came all over again.

With her hands on her hips and her voice loud enough for the whole world to hear, "Well, Sara, I guess you aren't a runner."

And that was that.

I wasn't a runner. For the next twenty-five years, I managed NOT to be a runner.

Through PE classes. Through gym memberships. Through chasing babies and toddlers and big kids.

But then it happened.

I had what we affectionately call a brain hiccup, a brief moment where the oxygen flow to my brain stopped and the left side of my body, weakened. Even though I did happen to score a snazzy cane as part of the deal, running became nearly impossible.

Strangely enough, from that moment on, all I could think about was running.

Running through my neighborhood. Running with my daughter who was training for a 5K. Running the Boston Marathon, for goodness sake.

I was obsessed with the very thing I had told myself I could never do because of one person's unthinking words. I had finally realized that a body that moves, no matter how fast or how slow, is an absolute gift. And I had to face the fact that I had let one moment steal the joy of living my best life.

In many ways, it was as though my heart had forgotten that my legs were made to run and jump and dance. It took a hiccup, a breath, a second to remind me that no matter my limitation, I am made to do hard things through the power of God's strength.

So, no matter what the world says you can't do, know He can restore you all the way to a dream fulfilled. It may be here as you persevere through the sting of harsh words or circumstances. Or it may be in heaven after a lifetime of strength gives way to the promise of forever.

But either way, know that someday *this* girl is going to shout for all eternity and the entire third grade to hear, "Watch out, y'all! I'm RUNNING to Jesus!!!!"

Truth Time:

Sometimes, it is difficult to truly grasp why God is so insistent about being careful with our words. But as in everything, His instruction comes from a place of love and a deep understanding of the human heart. God knows that when we use words without thinking, we can easily wound another person.

He speaks of this in Proverbs 12:18, "The words of the reckless pierce like swords, but the tongue of the wise brings healing."

Certainly, the teacher in our story spoke recklessly and in doing so, unknowingly planted a lie in my heart, a lie that I allowed to grow through my childhood and into my grown-up years. But there is no lie that God's truth can't conquer. And in my case, he used something hard to open my eyes and my heart to the power of Philippians 4:13, "For I can do all things through Christ who gives me strength."

It may seem at first that this simply means I can do whatever I set my mind to do because God is with me. But this truth runs so much deeper. Paul wrote these words while he was in jail, offering them to his friends at the church of Philippi so they would not be anxious or worry over his imprisonment.

And in Paul's offering, we are given the same hope. God will be with us in all things. Be it the good, the bad, or the in-between, He will stand beside us and give us strength so that we have the power to push one leg in front of the other and make it to the finish line.

So, remember, no matter the task in front of you, we were made to do hard things through the power of an almighty God. No words, no person, no one can *ever* take that away.

Girl Time:

Questions to ask your mom:

What lies from your childhood have you allowed yourself to believe?

What keeps you from exchanging them with God's truth?

Questions for your mom to ask you:

Tell me about a time when a grown-up's words made you feel badly about yourself. How can you use that experience to love others more intentionally with your own words?

Challenge Time:

After discussing the lies you both have allowed to take root in your hearts, write down five things God says about His children that counter those lies. Then, find a practical and purposeful way to overcome that lie. For me, I may not be able to run a 5K but I know that I want to walk one with my daughter no matter how slow I go!!!

Week 5

I am worth His time.

"God is the only one who will give us what our heart truly needs."

Reading Time:

The Lord is my shepherd, I lack nothing. He makes me lie down in green pastures, he leads me beside quiet waters, he refreshes my soul. He guides me along the right paths for his name's sake. Even though I walk through the darkest valley, I will fear no evil, for you are with me; your rod and your staff, they comfort me. You prepare a table before me in the presence of my enemies. You anoint my head with oil; my cup overflows. Surely your goodness and love will follow me all the days of my life, and I will dwell in the house of the Lord forever.

Psalm 23, NIV

Story Time with Brit:

It was one of those nights. A night when as soon as I sat down at my computer, I stared at my inbox for a good five minutes.

So many emails. So many questions. So many people needing something from me.

"I'll just answer a few," I thought as I glanced at the time.

But more than a few emails later, I felt a tug at my sleeve, "Mommy? Will you put me to bed?"

I glanced at the clock, knowing it was bedtime. So, I gently explained to my girl that I needed just five more minutes to finish an email and then I would be all hers. She nodded with a smile and left as quickly as she came.

A little while later, my boy found me and asked, "Mama, can you read me a story?" My answer was much the same as before except that five minutes had now become thirty. But I would be there soon.

Not long after he was gone, another little voice behind me said, "Mama, I want you to pray with me tonight." And with that, my heart *finally* heard what each little voice was trying to say with every sweet request.

My loves longed for my presence, my attention, my faith prayed over them. They needed only what I could give them. They needed *me.*

As I tucked each one of them in bed that night, I realized that in many ways, we are all like my babies, hungry for someone to be present in our lives. So, we will look to people to fill that need---a mom, a dad, a friend. But the truth is, God is the only one who will give us what our heart truly *needs and desires.*

Whenever we call, whenever we hurt, whenever life is overwhelming and cry, "Father?" He will be there. Ready to answer. Ready to love. Ready to accept us just as we are.

Not in an hour. Not in ten minutes. Not even in five.

He is ready now, always and forever.

Truth Time:

Every day, we seem to run around to the tune of busy-busy, rush-rush, and hurry-up.

Always moving. Always going. Always on to the next thing.

Sometimes, it may feel like no one sees us. But in everything and every way, God is perfectly present, ready to carry our hurt, listen to our cries and give us rest.

Remember David, the king from the Old Testament? As a young boy, David tended to his father's sheep. It was out of this experience that he no doubt wrote Psalm 23, beginning with, "The Lord is my shepherd; I have all that I need. He lets me rest in green meadows; he leads me beside peaceful streams. He renews my strength."

In calling Him Shepherd, David is saying that God is our Father, Counselor, Provider, and Best Friend. He is the one we can turn to when life overwhelms. He will help us to be still so that He can bring peace to our weary hearts and restoration to our souls.

Not only will He be there when we reach out but He will also find us when we are lost and forget our way back to Him.

Our Father, like the shepherd, will leave the 99 to find the one lost sheep (Luke 15:4.) He will leave His entire flock alone to find the one that has wandered away, the one who is in trouble, the one who is hurt and cannot make it back on her own. He loves us THAT much.

So never wait to cry out, call out, reach out to the One who will always be who we need when we need Him.

No matter when. No matter where. No matter what.

Girl Time:

Questions to ask your mom:

Do you feel you're distracted by life's demands? Do you ever feel like your prayers are not good enough for God? Why or why not?

Questions for your mom to ask you:

Do you think that God wants to spend time with you? Why or why not?

Challenge Time:

Read the rest of Psalm 23. Write it in your own words. Post it on a mirror in the bathroom you see every day as a reminder that God cares and wants to hear from you always.

Week 6

I am a masterpiece.

"We are His best work, His highest thought, and His most persistent act of love."

Reading Time:

For we are God's masterpiece. He has created us anew in Christ Jesus, so we can do the good things he planned for us long ago.

Ephesians 2:10, NLV

Story Time with Sara:

When I picture my daddy in my growing-up years, I see the two of us, hand-in-hand, walking through the halls of our local museum.

Each visit we'd follow the same, sweet routine---making our way through the exhibits, eating lunch in the beautiful courtyard, and shopping at the gift shop for "just a little something."

Although time may have taken my memories of the galleries he loved, the lovely things we ate, and the "little somethings" I received, there is one day I will never forget.

I was standing at the bottom of a stairwell looking up at the biggest Buddha I'd ever seen when I asked, "Daddy, who on earth would call that art?"

He smiled gently, as was his way, and said, "Because someone saw its beauty and called it so."

I stood there for a minute thinking about my answer and then my belly's growl reminded me that it was time for lunch. So off we went to food nearly too beautiful to eat. And as we sat down, I had almost put that Buddha out of my mind when my daddy said quietly:

"We are all like that Buddha, Sara. Our Father is the artist, sculpting and knitting us together in such a way that each of us is one of a kind. And in our crafting, He sees beauty and calls us so. That kind of beauty transcends time just like the art in this museum. It is unchanged even when everything else fades away."

And in that moment, I began to understand something great from a man who usually said very little. I was beautiful because the God of the universe had called me so. As I have grown, this truth has echoed into my heart over and over and over again.

When I've looked in the mirror and struggled with what I see. When my body has changed in ways that frustrate me. When the world has tried to break me down and tear me apart.

In each and every moment, it is as though my daddy is there, reminding me of my Father's heart, "Remember you *are* beautiful because I have called you so."

Truth Time:

Imagine all the things it takes for an artist to create a true masterpiece.

Thought. Time. Energy. Emotion. Talent. Persistence.

It all comes together to give the world something beautiful and something that reflects the hands and heart that made it.

Our God's work is no different. Isaiah 64:8 says, "You are our Father, we are the clay and You, our potter. All of us are a work of Your hand." You can trust that God is molding you, shaping you, growing you into a beautiful one-of-a-kind masterpiece.

There may be days we doubt it.

We may hear words from another that tear us down. Or we may even hear our own voices saying, "If only I looked like her..." "If only I could do the things she does..." On and on until we forget that we are unique on purpose.

But His Word is there to remind us, "For we are God's masterpiece. He created us anew in Christ Jesus so we can do the good things He planned for us long ago." Ephesians 2:10

Let's allow that truth wash over us.

We are each a unique work of art, made beautiful and called so by the very God who created it all. We are like clay in His hand, crafted with His purpose and renewed in Jesus. We are His best work, His highest thought, His most persistent act of love.

We are masterpieces, dear ones.

Woven together by the heart and hand of God to give the world His one and only you.

Girl Time:

Questions to ask your mom:

When God calls you a masterpiece, do you believe Him? Why or why not?

Questions for your mom to ask you:

How can knowing that God calls us all His masterpiece help you and I see the beauty in each other?

Challenge Time:

Find a work of art (either online or in a museum) that is considered a masterpiece. Talk about why it is worthy of that name and why God might call you the same.

Week 7

I am seen.

"We are chosen.
We are loved.
We are written on the
palm of His hand."

Reading Time:

See, I have marked your names on My hands. Your walls are always before Me.

Isaiah 49:16, NLV

Story Time with Brit:

"God sees you, Eli. He's written your name on the palm of His Hand. And you are His forever."

My boy's big brown eyes looked up at me as I spoke these words over him.

Words that came without effort because they were given to someone I loved. Words that spoke of my longing for him to believe and know that God sees him always. Words I had struggled to accept myself.

Because I was the girl who always felt out of place, who carried a permanent question mark.

Am I pretty enough? Am I thin enough? Am I wearing the right clothes? Do people like me? Do people approve of me? Do people love me for me?

Snuggled up next to my boy, I felt so many of those questions filling my heart once again even as I spoke of God's promises. But as if he knew my doubt, Eli jumped down, grabbed a permanent marker and wrote his name on my hand with a little heart right beside it and then did the same on his own.

I smiled at his sweet understanding of the truth I'd spoken over him, a truth I had needed to hear myself. So, I took the marker and wrote my name on my other hand as a visual reminder that I am who God says I am.

I am chosen. I am loved. I am written on the palm of His hand.

It is a truth that is more than a Sunday. It is the everyday promise of a loving God who begs us to listen to voice. Because He knows if we depend on what the world says, we will be left disappointed.

But if we hold onto His promises, our doubts will be erased by the very breath of God, leaving our hearts open and free to accept the truth with which we began...

"God sees you. He's written your name on the palm of His hand. And you are His forever."

Truth Time:

We all want to be loved and accepted.

Be it by our friends, our family or our community. As precious as those relationships may become, the truth is that those things will fade and fail us. But the words God speaks over us are forever true.

"See, I have engraved you on the palms of my hands..." Isaiah 49:16a

When Eli wrote his name on my hand, I could not keep it from my gaze. I constantly saw it so he was never far from my mind. In the same way, God has our names permanently written on His hand so we can be assured that we will never be forgotten.

Too many of us are walking around vulnerable to the lie that unless we fit in, we are invisible.

So, we desperately strive for approval instead of holding on to the truth of Galatians 1:10: *Am I trying to win the approval of men, or of God? Or am I trying to please people? If I were still trying to please people, I would not be a servant of Christ.*

It is in this striving that we forget the grace of God and what love it took for Him to give His Son so we could be free.

Yes, we all want to be loved. Yes, we all want to be accepted. Yes, we all want to fit in.

But if we still our hearts, we are free to receive the truth that once we've been accepted by the God of the universe, we can never be rejected.

Girl Time:

Questions to ask your mom:

What is one thing you do to fit in with other moms? Does that allow you the freedom to be who God created you to be?

Questions for your mom to ask you:

What is one thing you do to fit-in with other girls? Does that one thing get in the way of who God made you to be?

Challenge Time:

Write your name with a permanent marker on the palm of your hand. At the end of the week, share with each other how the exercise helped you both remember that God sees you always.

Week 8

I am loved by a God who heals.

"I will never forget the moment I heard her say, 'I know it's hard but sometimes you need to distance yourself from toxic people and remember who God says you are.'"

Reading Time:

He heals the heartbroken and bandages their wounds.

Psalm 147:3, The Message

Story Time with Sara:

"Oh no, Mommy, you have a boo boo!!!"

I watched my baby girl's eyes widen as she pointed to the marks on the small of my back. So, I pulled her close and assured her, "It's okay, sweets. Mommy's boo boo is much better. This mark just says that I used to have a boo boo."

Those big eyes searched my face for a moment, looked at the boo boo one more time and then turned back to the pile of treasures she had been putting into her Barbie purse. But as my gaze returned to the mirror, I couldn't help but take inventory of my boo boo-scars.

The ones on my back that had drawn my girl's attention, ugly but purposeful, holding in a machine that makes life a little easier. The ones on my belly, from having babies and the toll weight of what it took to get them here. The ones on my hands, testament to my forgetfulness and not-so-fine motor skills.

And then, there were the ones that are harder to find---the ones you wouldn't even know were there, etched in my heart from all the hard things that life sometimes brings.

Yes, the world would say I have many scars.

But even as I realize that some might call them ugly and even as I know there are probably more to come, I see only healing. I see the ugly beautiful truth that God can heal all my broken places with the grace of His love.

Because my scars, the visible, the invisible and even the yet-to-be prove that Jesus is in the business of making me new. Each one, made more beautiful by the grace tucked so carefully inside it. Each one, made more meaningful by the story it quietly tells.

It is this beauty, this faithfulness, this meaning that sings in every crooked mark we carry. It says we have journeyed through both peaks and valleys. But it also shouts with the power of the God of the universe that we have been forever healed.

Truth Time:

Sometimes, it is hard to see beauty in a world that is broken.

We may be quick to call it ugly and mean and hopeless especially when we have been hurt.

But the truth is, Jesus came to save the broken and bring hope to the hopeless. And a beautiful part of that plan is that He has given us who know Him an incredible way to share His love through hard things.

"For we are God's instruments to do his work and speak out for him, to tell others of the night-and-day difference he made for us–from nothing to something, from rejected to accepted." (I Peter 2:9-10)

Our pain, our scars, our stories are a way for us to show another, "I have been there too."

Even His scars, born out of His greatest pain on the Cross allowed the world to recognize who Jesus was and the miracle of His resurrection. His story made all that was ugly about them, beautiful. His healing made it possible to see that death had finally been defeated and He paved a way for our own stories of healing to do the same.

In my own life, I have watched the grace of Psalm 147:3 wash over me as well as those I love, "He is near to the broken hearted and binds up their wounds." Over and over and over again, God has drawn close to our broken places while He works to mend and restore them.

Not terribly long ago, I saw this mending in my daughter as she was being bullied by another girl.

This girl had said unkind things and spread rumors about her even though my daughter had been nothing but kind. I watched as my daughter went from confident to visibly beaten overnight. For nearly a month, it seemed as though there was no way out.

We prayed. We sought counsel. We read truth.

But then one day, I saw the confidence in my girl begin to return. It was not long after that I heard her talking on the phone to one of her friends. She was sharing her story, her hard, her experience because her friend was going through something similar.

I will never forget the moment I heard her say, "I know it's hard but sometimes you need to distance yourself from toxic people and remember who God says you are."

This is the beauty of allowing God to mend what is broken in us.

The marks left behind tell a story.

A story that says that no matter what is broken, God can heal it all the way to beautiful.

Girl Time:

Questions to ask your mom:

What part of your story has God used to help others? Explain.

Questions for your mom to ask you:

Do you have any scars? If so, what did you learn from the healing process? How do you think God might use it to help others going through something similar?

Challenge Time:

Tell a story either out-loud or written-down with the purpose of letting someone know she is not alone. Find ways and opportunities to use that story this week.

Week 9

I am strong.

"In every circumstance, in every challenge, in every uncertainty, Jesus will love us all the way to knowing, 'With God all things are possible.'"

Reading Time:

You are my strength, I sing praise to you; you, God, are my fortress, my God on whom I can rely.

Psalm 59:17, NIV

Story Time with Brit:

I walked into the school gym with my head hung low and my step, uncertain.

Uncertain because somewhere between my fuzzy hair and crooked teeth, I had convinced myself I was unwanted. It was as though each step drew me further into who I thought I was instead of who I knew God made me to be.

I was shy. I was awkward. I was lonely. And I desperately wanted to fit in with everyone else.

But just as I began to also mourn my not-so-stylish clothes, my coach announced, "It's time for some kickball!" An announcement that made my head hang even lower because I knew what came next.

Captains would be picked. Teams would be chosen. And my name would be called last.

All I could do was find a corner, sink to the floor, and think, "Nobody wants me on their team. Nobody will ever pick me because I am not the popular girl." Back and forth I went---from nobody this to nobody that---until I caught her out of the corner of my eye.

There in the middle of it all, my coach had noticed me and was now walking towards me.

With a gentle voice and a quiet grace, she sat down beside me and began to tell me how important I was to this game, how God had given me unique abilities, and how my classmates should be proud to have me on their team.

Then she added with a smile, "And you can kick harder than any of those boys too!"

With that, my face lit up and suddenly my heart felt encouraged and my soul, confident. All because my coach took the time to see me, know me, and encourage me. Even now, her words inspire me.

I still may feel out of place. I still may not look like other girls. I still may be a little awkward.

But if I hold onto His promises, I can trust that God has made me for an important purpose. I can know He has gifted me with unique abilities. And I can have confidence that He will give me the strength to do what He can only do through me.

Truth Time:

Sometimes, the strength we need seems so far away.

Maybe our hearts hurt. Maybe our bodies ache. Maybe our minds feel jumbled.

But just as my coach came alongside me in love, Jesus is always ready to come alongside us and show us how God's strength will always be enough.

In every circumstance, in every challenge, in every uncertainty, Jesus will love us all the way to knowing, "With God all things are possible." (Matthew 19:26)

Even when we feel alone in a room full of people, Jesus will be the best friend we will ever have. He will dry our tears in the bad times. He will dance with us in the good times. And just like my coach, He will never be afraid to walk our way and sit in our sadness.

But that isn't where His love ends.

Jesus lived and died to show us the power of a good and faithful friend so that we can then extend that friendship to others who are feeling lost and alone. We are made to encourage one another, to build each other up. (I Thessalonians 5:11) We are designed to be His hands and feet, helping one another to get back into the game.

In many ways, Jesus is asking us to be the someone who reaches out to the girl in the corner.

He asks us to encourage her. He asks us to love her. He asks us to remind her of her strength.

So that when the world makes her question it, she can have the confidence to answer back, "My God is my strength. My God is my fortress. My God is my portion. And He will give me the strength to do what He can only do through me."

Girl Time:

Questions to ask your mom:

Describe a moment when you have felt left out but the kindness of someone else helped you to realize you had the strength to face it.

Questions for your mom to ask you:

Describe a time when you reached out to someone who didn't seem to quite fit in.

Challenge Time:

Craft a letter of encouragement to the girl in the corner *together.* Make sure to include any scripture/words that would have encouraged your heart if you had been in her shoes.

Week 10

I am free to be me.

"We will all struggle to fit in. We will all face embarrassing moments. We will all feel the discomfort of being in a new place or new season of life. But we were never meant to face it alone."

Reading Time:

Before I shaped you in the womb, I knew all about you. Before you saw the light of day, I had holy plans for you: a prophet to the nations—that's what I had in mind for you.

Jeremiah 1:5, The Message

Story Time with Sara:

I remember it like it was yesterday.

The pool. The kid. The lifeguard.

I remember it all.

There I was just a young mama of two desperately trying to keep both of my babies alive at the local pool when my one-year-old son shouts, "I slide! I slide!!!"

I'll admit I was a little over-protective. But it seemed completely reasonable for me to put my baby on my lap and try the slide together. After all, there was a treacherous six-inch pool of water at the bottom!?!?!

Okay, so maybe it only *seemed* treacherous at the time.

But nevertheless, I scooped up my boy, sat him on my lap and off we went...

Until we didn't.

Apparently, my grown-up backside was too big for a slide made for babies.

I mean, who *knew?*

A fact that was made even more obvious by the lifeguard who was running towards me, frantically blowing his whistle. At first, I thought, "Oh, what a sweet darling boy coming to my rescue!" Sweet and darling until he said loudly for all the world to hear, "Adults are not allowed to slide down this slide!"

And now the entire pool need only to observe the woman stuck in the slide to know why.

So, I did what any rational girl would do---I started laughing so hard I could barely breathe with a hyena sound snort that could be heard for miles.

Startled and left with no other option but to help, the lifeguard along with TWO OTHER LIFEGUARDS freed my behind from the clutches of the slide and the day, er, the bum was saved.

As for me, I wisely chose to wait four years and two kids later to return to said pool.

But the point of sharing this ill-fated pool visit?

Life is filled with embarrassing moments.

Some will be mercifully private. Some will be kindly in front of people who love you. And yes, some will unfortunately be in front of what feels like the entire world.

But do not lose heart.

For the moments that bring tears, He is there to dry them. For the moments that bring humiliation, He is there to trade it for freedom. For the moments that are just ridiculous, He gives you laughter.

And if you are really blessed like me, He brings 3 lifeguards to save you too.

Truth Time:

For years, I thought that embarrassing, red-faced moments and the hurt that came with them weren't big enough for God.

It was as though I believed He would see them as unworthy or if I cried out for help, He would say, "I'm sorry, Sara. I have somewhere else to be." It was even as if the pain of feeling awkward or humiliated or left out wasn't real.

But the truth is, every girl in every phase of her life will feel this kind of pain.

We will all struggle to fit in. We will all face embarrassing moments. We will all feel the discomfort of being in a new place or new season of life.

But we were never meant to face it alone.

God wants to face our hurt with us. God wants to answer our cries for help. God wants you to know the confidence of Psalm 71:2: "Because you are right and good, take me out of trouble. Turn your ear and save me."

When David wrote this cry for help, he was an old man and had experienced a lifetime of God's faithfulness. He knew that no matter what the circumstance God would come. He knew that when his heart hurt God cared. And he knew that even in his imperfection God loved him and wanted the best for him.

We can claim David's trust in a faithful God just as confidently when hurtful things happen as a part of an imperfect world.

But even in those things, God wants to come to our rescue by wrapping us up in the safety of His grace. And He also wants to give us peace in knowing that before we were even shaped in the womb, He knew us, He had plans for us, and He wanted to tell His story through us (Jeremiah 1:5.)

Because our God is not in the business of hurt and humiliation. (So, be careful of those who say He is.) He is instead the safe place in which to land when those things come.

So, let's allow God to love us in *all things* because at the end of the day, He doesn't want our perfection. He wants our broken and our messy. He wants our hard and hilarious. He wants our happy and our sad.

He wants it all, girls.

Because He knows us, He has plans for us, and He is telling His story through us one messy, glorious step at a time.

Girl Time:

Questions to ask your mom:

Tell me about a time when you were embarrassed. Does that moment still hurt or have you let God carry it and you?

Questions for your mom to ask you:

Describe a time when someone you loved was embarrassed. Did you try to make them feel better by coming to their rescue? Why or why not?

Challenge Time:

Identify one person in your life who has been singled out and picked on. How can you come to his/her defense? How can you show love to him/her in a practical and purposeful way?

Week 11

I am held.

"He is hope when we have none, He is strength when we are weak, and He is peace when our hearts are broken."

Reading Time:

For I hold you by your right hand– I, the Lord your God. And I say to you, "Don't be afraid. I am here to help you."

Isaiah 41:13, NLT

Story Time with Brit:

My hands shook wildly as I pulled my car over to catch my breath.

Something in my heart was ripped open as I pushed through my workout at the gym. The news that a dear friend had lost her father felt fresh again. And tears began to fall so quickly that I didn't notice my hands shaking until I had already left the parking lot.

My heart ached for her and in its aching, I knew I needed to sit awhile and let the sadness wash over me. So, I found an empty parking lot and rested under the weight of my hurt for my friend and the physical hurt from my workout.

It was there in my car, hands shaking, heart pounding, tears falling, I heard my trainer's words that morning echo in my head,

"You can do this. Get up. Keep going. You've got this in you, girl. I know this is hard---what you are doing is hard. But get up because I am right here to help you. Get up because I am here to encourage you. Get up because you can do this."

And in every word, I heard another voice, *His voice*, reminding me of His presence in all things.

Even when we get devastating news that leaves us face down on the floor and thinking we can't get up again, He is there. Even when we are beat up and so heartbroken over all that life can bring our way, He is there. Even when life throws a sucker punch we never saw coming, He is there.

Even when, He is there.

In disappointment. In hurt. In sickness. In pain.

Jesus is there saying, "Come, climb into my lap and let me hold you. I am here. I am always here."

All you need to do is look up and take His hand.

Because He is hope when we have none, He is strength when we are weak, and He is peace when our hearts are broken. He is enough.

He will *always* be enough.

Truth Time:

Life is full of hard things.

Things that will sometimes be difficult to understand. Things that make us question and wonder why. Things that will hurt our hearts so deeply our bodies shake.

But no matter the hard thing, Isaiah 41:3 holds us up in hope, "I am the Lord your God who takes hold of your right hand and says to you, 'Do not fear, I will help you.'"

Take a moment to let that truly sink in. The God of the universe, the Maker of all we see is there to hold our hands and help us through all our hard things.

When we fall, He says, "You can do this. Get up. Keep going. You've got this in you, girl."

When we hurt, He says, "I know this is hard---what you are doing is hard. But get up because I am right here to help you. Get up because I am here to encourage you. Get up because you can do this."

When we doubt, He says, "Come climb upon my lap and let me hold you. I am here. I am always here."

Our pain and the pain of this world breaks His heart and we will find because it breaks His, it will break ours.

We will not be able to stand by when we see someone hurting or broken because we know how it feels to have the very hand of God holding ours in our hardest moments.

Galatians 6:2 says to "bear one another's burdens" which is the call for us to not only lean into the hope of an ever-present, loving God but to also carry others hurt in the way God has carried our own.

So that in moments where others fall or hurt or doubt, we can be the hand that reaches out and the voice that says, "I know this is hard--- what you are doing is hard. But get up because I am right here to help you. Get up because I am here to encourage you. Get up, strong girl, because you can do this."

All because He first held *us.*

Girl Time:

Questions to ask your mom:

Describe a moment where you felt the world has knocked you down.

Were you able to trust that God was with you in that moment? Why or why not?

Questions for your mom to ask you:

Has there ever been a time that you have seen someone else hurting? What did you do? What do you think God would have wanted you to do in that same situation?

Challenge Time:

Choose one person in your life you know needs encouragement. Do some mom-daughter brainstorming to figure out how you can purposefully encourage this person and be the one to stand at the sidelines and say, "You can do this! Keep going! You've got this!"

Week 12

I am made to love well.

"We were never made to chase a beautiful picture. We were made to chase a beautiful heart."

Reading Time:

For the Lord does not look at the things people look at. People look at the outward appearance, but the Lord looks at the heart.

I Samuel 16:7, NIV

Story Time with Sara:

The minute I saw her reflection, I saw myself.

The wrinkle in her nose. The crease in her forehead. The slump in her shoulder.

All coming together to reveal the insecurity I had so often seen in my own face as I stood in front of the mirror. So, with all the love I could muster, I put my arms around my girl and whispered softly in her ear, "You are absolutely beautiful."

A look of relief came over her face as she turned back to take another glance at her new glasses. Then with a shrug and a half-smile, she jumped down from her chair, leaving the doctor's office with her hand in mine.

And that was that.

Until somewhere in the hustle and bustle of the first day of school, it wasn't.

Catching her reflection in the bathroom mirror, I noticed the wrinkle in her nose had returned. But this time, there was also a sadness in her eyes. So, I offered up a little, "You okay?"

"No, mom. I'm just so afraid all the kids in my class will say mean things about my glasses."

My heart fell as she looked at me for some kind of reassurance. So, with my arms around her, I gave her all I had in a prayer for her heart. And then I let her go.

Let her go until the van door opened that afternoon.

It was as everyone piled in, I heard my girl's voice above the rest, "Mom, someone said I was goofy-looking." And after I whispered an "I'm so sorry," I asked my normally outspoken girl, "And what did you say back?"

"Nothing."

"Really???"

"Yup. I mean, I was really mad. Like crazy mad, Mom. So, I knew if I said anything it might be something that would make his heart hurt. I just knew I didn't want his heart to feel as badly as mine did."

As I sat there in the echo of her words, I felt tears begin to fall.

Fall at her strength to turn away from an angry reply. Fall at the Jesus-sized love it took for her to choose compassion. Fall at the way my little morning-time prayer had been answered.

Because somewhere in between the doctor's office and the minivan, my girl had found that true beauty is not a reflection in a mirror but is instead, a reflection of the heart.

Truth Time:

In a culture of selfies and social media, it seems almost impossible for a girl to escape her own reflection.

We find ourselves adding filters, changing angles, snapping shot after shot in the hope that one will be good enough for the world to see. But when it comes down to it, we are chasing something that can never be caught. We are chasing perfection.

But. Girls.

We were never made to chase a beautiful picture. We were made to chase a beautiful heart.

"For the Lord does not look at the things people look at. People look at the outward appearance, but the Lord looks at the heart." (I Samuel 16:7)

To know this truth is one thing but to live it out is another.

In a world so focused on image, it can be easy to strive for someone else's approval. And in that striving, it can be even easier to forget to grow your heart by loving well, especially when you have been hurt by another's unkind words.

That is why it could have been very easy for my girl to have met her classmate's unkindness with unkindness. But instead, she chose love. And in doing so, she chose the beauty of a growing heart.

In the same way, God is asking us all to grow by loving well. "For the entire law is fulfilled in keeping one command, 'Love your neighbor as yourself.'" (Galatians 5:14) And although we can show love in what we do, we can also show love in what we say.

Sometimes that means silence and the wisdom to know when to walk away. Sometimes that means thinking about another person's heart before you speak. And sometimes that means standing up to unkind words out of love for someone else or even yourself.

But we cannot do it in our own strength.

We need His grace. We need His mercy. We need His heart. We need a love that says, "Forgive." When the crowd says, "Crucify."

Because a love like that can change the world.

Girl Time

Questions to ask your mom:

Tell me about a time someone said something unkind to you about your appearance and you responded in kindness. Tell me about a time someone said something unkind to you about your appearance and you responded unkindly. Explain why you think you reacted differently to each situation.

Questions for your mom to ask you:

Have you ever had someone speak unkindly to you about your appearance? How did it make you feel? What did you say back to him/her? How do you think what you said made him/her feel?

Challenge Time:

Identify one person you have treated unkindly. Pick one way you can encourage this person's heart this week---a note, a phone call, etc. and do it!

Meet Our Contributors

Brittany Frey (Author) is the owner and founder of *Truth Ink*, a faith-based clothing company in Southlake, Texas. She is passionate about teaching the next generation of women to intimately know God through the truth of His word and the gift of His Son. Her previous book, *Cover Them*, was released in 2017. And when she isn't designing t-shirts, drinking coffee, or at the gym, you will find this self-expressed mess raising her three babies with her husband, Patrick, in Colleyville, Texas..

Sara Cormany (Author) is mama to four beautiful babies and wife to one sweet man. She is a writer, a speaker, a teacher, a chronic illness ninja, and a champion nose wiper. But her most cherished role is being one who is held, loved, and known by Jesus. She loves watching Him take the messy and mundane of life and turn it into something beautiful.

Meet Our Contributors

Christine Gervasini (Graphic Designer) is a calligrapher and lettering artist with a love of typography and all related forms of design. She currently enjoys designing for Truth Ink Apparel where she cannot only share her work, but her faith as well. She lives in Rhode Island with her husband, Andrew, and Golden Retriever, Marvel.

18557741R00088

Made in the USA
Lexington, KY
22 November 2018